Birding Babylon

Birding Babylon

A Soldier's Journal from Iraq

Jonathan Trouern-Trend

SIERRA CLUB BOOKS
San Francisco

The Sierra Club, founded in 1892 by John Muir, has devoted itself to the study and protection of the earth's scenic and ecological resources—mountains, wetlands, woodlands, wild shores and rivers, deserts and plains. The publishing program of the Sierra Club offers books to the public as a nonprofit educational service in the hope that they may enlarge the public's understanding of the Club's basic concerns. The point of view expressed in each book, however, does not necessarily represent that of the Club. The Sierra Club has some sixty chapters throughout the United States. For information about how you may participate in its programs to preserve wilderness and the quality of life, please address inquiries to Sierra Club, 85 Second Street, San Francisco, California 94105, or visit our website at www.sierraclub.org.

Published by Sierra Club Books
85 Second Street, San Francisco, CA 94105
www.sierraclub.org/books

Produced and distributed by
University of California Press
Berkeley and Los Angeles, California
University of California Press, Ltd.
London, England
www.ucpress.edu

SIERRA CLUB, SIERRA CLUB BOOKS, and the Sierra Club design logos are registered trademarks of the Sierra Club.

We are grateful to Christopher Helm Publishers for permission to adapt artwork copyright © 1996 by A. Birch, J. Gale, M. Langman, and B. Small, from *Birds of the Middle East* (Princeton Field Guides), by R. F. Porter, S. Christensen, and P. Schiermacker-Hansen. All rights reserved.

Library of Congress Cataloging-in-Publication data is available upon request from the publisher.

ISBN-10 1-57805-131-2

ISBN-13 978-1-57805-131-1

Printed in china

Printed in the United States of America on acid-free paper

13 12 11 10 09 08 07 06

10 9 8 7 6 5 4 3 2

To my wife, Nancy, and my children,
Alexander, Rebecca, Christopher, Jennifer, and Elizabeth

CONTENTS

PREFACE

I've often been struck by how differently people see the same place. A photographer sees the world in terms of contrasts and composition. An architect sees it in terms of space and structure. In Iraq there are ten thousand ways to see the world. I consider myself lucky to have seen it through the eyes of a naturalist.

When I think of my time in Iraq, my thoughts turn first to the good things: my friends, both Iraqi and American, and my time observing wildlife. Though my medical unit saw the terrible face of war, I also discovered a country rich in history and natural beauty, where I could pursue my lifelong passion for nature. Iraq is full of people who love the natural world, with whom I felt a natural kinship, who would bring me insects or talk with me about birds and their names and where they could be found.

I was fortunate to be stationed on one of the largest American bases, Camp Anaconda, north of Baghdad in the Sunni Triangle. Its 15 square miles held not only a large portion of the American arsenal in Iraq but also many birds and other creatures that shared the base with us. Though it was a hive of military activity and a target of almost daily rocket and mortar attacks, it was also a refuge of sublime natural beauty to those who looked. My job in our battalion intelligence section also allowed me to travel to other parts of the country, from the sparse deserts of Al-Anbar Province to the awe-inspiring ruins of Babylon and Ur to the palaces and urban streets of Baghdad.

When I started my online journal *Birding Babylon*, shortly after arriving, I got significantly more response than expected. In retrospect it should have been no surprise. Most people's view of life in Iraq focuses on the chaos and violence of war. To read about something as universally familiar as the migration of birds, or watching ducks in a pond, fulfilled a need to know that something worthwhile or even magical was happening, even in the midst of suicide bombings and rocket attacks. I believe this is why I received so many comments, some recounting how they cried—maybe not knowing exactly why—when they read about my often-mundane birding on base. Knowing that the great cycles of nature continue despite what people happen to be doing is reassuring, I think. There is an order we can take comfort in and draw strength from.

For me, the familiar took the form of birds I knew from back home or from my time in Europe. The first ducks I saw, a flock of shovelers, could just as easily have been seen in Connecticut. The barn swallows migrating over our

Kuwaiti staging area reminded me of those I could find at our town lake in early April. The wood pigeons and coots on base were identical to the birds I had seen at St. James Park in London. Even the ubiquitous house sparrows, residents of every McDonald's in America, were with me in the most remote desert outpost. The birds gave me both the excitement of the new and exotic (as with the hoopoe) and the anchor of the familiar. In the predictable migrations of shorebirds, followed by the land birds and waterfowl, I found continuity and reassurance.

There are soldiers in every war who have the naturalist's eye. A foreign land is fertile ground for the curious. I knew a World War II veteran who spent time in the Pacific islands catching lizards and insects and sending specimens to the Smithsonian in Washington. Since returning from Iraq I've found that I was not alone as a birder there. I know of at least a dozen marines, soldiers, airmen, and civilians from several countries who brought their binoculars to war. They share information with me as I continue to write about Iraq's birds and other wildlife online. I try to make the blog a place where people can read firsthand observations from the ground and about international efforts to help the birds. My archive of postings from Iraq is also there (*http://birdingbabylon.blogspot.com*). The ones chosen for this book have been edited for publication.

What most excites me is learning that Iraqi birders have begun surveying the birds of the southern marshes. Life is returning to some of the ruined areas, and some species feared extinct have been seen. To me this is emblematic of the resiliency of life, of both birds and people, in the face of crisis.

I hope to return to Iraq one day armed only with binoculars and camera. Perhaps an Iraqi friend and I will drive around searching the deserts, the river valleys, the marshes, and the mountains for the birds I missed. We will talk about how wonderful it is to be free of the fences and able to go where the birds are instead of hoping they'll fly into our compound. No matter how long it takes to get to that future, I know the birds will be waiting.

Jonathan Trouern-Trend
Marlborough, Connecticut

I'm a soldier in Iraq. I've been mobilized for up to 18 months, which includes a definite 12 months in Iraq and Kuwait. I have been birding since I was 12 years old, which makes it 24 years now. I'm in a New England medical unit. I plan to write about my nature observations during my time here, both birds and other critters.

I've got to get back to work now.

I landed in Kuwait in the middle of the night the first week of February, after spending two months training in an ungodly cold Army base in the States. It was a splendid way to train for the desert.

Birding in Kuwait was limited due to my location in the middle of nowhere, surrounded by thousands of coalition troops coming or going to Iraq. During my two-week stay, I'm sorry to say that I saw only 5 species—house sparrow, barn swallow, rock dove, desert wheatear, and crested lark. Driving down the highway near Kuwait City there were many places that looked very good for birds but alas, I was driving in a convoy. Maybe next time.

The crested larks have turned out to be one of the most common birds, in both Kuwait and Iraq. They are a bit bigger and plumper than a horned lark and have a funny little crest on their head that always seems to be sticking straight up. They run a few feet, stop and look around, then repeat this—all day long.

Our convoy up from Kuwait had to stop because one of the humvees had a flat. We all piled out of the vehicles and set up a defensive perimeter with our weapons pointing out. It was a bit of a surreal scene: I'm lying on the ground with my eye on some guy racing around in a pickup truck, wondering if he's going to take a potshot at us (which would have been suicidal), while a pair of crested larks were not even 10 feet from me, the male displaying and dancing around.

Around 3:00 a.m. we crossed the border into Iraq. By the time it was light, we were far into the country. In the south the landscape was like Kuwait, flat desert with a cast of green from the winter rains. There were a few camels and traditional black Bedouin tents here and there with large flocks of sheep and goats nearby.

We drove through the southern marshes, which were absolutely decimated by Saddam's draining program to destroy the traditional home of the Marsh Arabs. All along the road were ditches and dug up ground. For miles and miles the land looked like a giant disorganized construction zone.

As we moved north the desert became scrub. We got off the highway and onto a dirt road to avoid the populated areas. What looked like miles from any dwellings little kids stood by the side of the road waving to us.

I was surprised to see pools of water all along the roadside. The birding was fantastic. I haven't had so many life birds in one day since being in Indonesia in 1990. There were birds everywhere, waterbirds and shorebirds in the pools, land birds flying by or sitting on fences. The number (I saw 26 species that day) was in stark contrast to the dearth of birds in Kuwait.

The pools had so many shorebirds that I could only identify the large and distinctive ones as we whizzed by. There were lots of black-winged stilts, avocets, red-wattled plover, and black-headed gulls. Lots of hooded crows and rooks.

Yesterday I had a little time in the morning and took a three-hour walk around the base. A few migrants are moving through. In the last few weeks I've seen black redstart, some unidentified *Phylloscopus* warbler, white wagtail, barn swallows, European goldfinches, and chaffinches. At a lagoon on the other side of the base I saw 25 shovelers (ducks) and a couple of redshanks.

Slowly I'm getting to know the better birding areas on the base. I found that by going behind one of the buildings I got a great view of a little lagoon surrounded by phragmites reeds. About 50 wood pigeons were sitting in dead trees around the lagoon. These birds winter here in large numbers, and I expect them to be leaving north soon. In the lagoon I saw a couple of coots, three moorhens chasing each other in the grass, a magpie flying over the marsh, and a spectacular purple swamphen. Swallows were wheeling around over the water catching insects.

I saw some behavior I had never seen before.

High in the air, probably 1,000 feet up, a small group of rooks was riding a thermal just like they were a kettle of broad-winged hawks. They moved up the rising air effortlessly, wheeling around, then at the top they glided away at a fast clip. The rooks are everywhere in the farmland surrounding my base, looking for food in the freshly plowed soil. Many of them will also be moving north.

Tomorrow I get to go on a run to the burn pit. We throw our garbage into a trailer and haul it off to a giant pile of burning trash. Though it's over a mile away, every day we see a giant plume of smoke. Some days the wind blows it in our direction and a haze descends on our living area. Sometimes little pieces of burnt paper rain down from the sky. I'm looking forward to going, even though I'll probably have to change my uniform and take a shower afterward. The dump is a big draw to gulls and crows, and I'm sure I'll see something good in the gull department.

Today I had to drive some people over to get a helicopter ride, so I took my binos and bird book. On the way I saw a nice lesser kestrel fly right in front of my humvee. In an open field across the street from the burn pit I counted approximately 575 black-headed gulls in various stages of molt. About half had their summer plumage. While I was watching, a C-130 flying low overhead deployed flares and did an evasive maneuver. I didn't see any smoke trail of an antiaircraft missile (looks like a tight corkscrew), so it may have been a false alarm.

On the fences I saw a male chaffinch and a common babbler. The latter bird was a lifer, and it was very cooperative while I watched it.

Birding on base doesn't usually elicit any undue attention from the MPs. I think everyone thinks I'm doing security work when I'm looking into the distance with binoculars. I'm not sure what they think when I'm looking up in a tree.

Last Saturday I went on a short walk around the living areas with one of our doctors. In some large eucalyptus trees we saw a small group of white-cheeked bulbuls. One of the birds was displaying—lowering its head, drooping its wings, and fanning its tail. We also saw collared doves, wood pigeons, barn swallows, and a red-wattled plover.

After I dropped the doc off at the clinic and drove to another vantage point, I saw a summer-plumage whiskered tern cruising over the water. This was a lifer and a very significant one to me. The bird looks like a common tern with a dark breast. They are a marsh tern, like the black tern. In the summer of 1993 I drove to Delaware twice to look for the first North American record of this species, but was skunked both times. (The trip did produce a sharp-tailed sandpiper and some great butterflies.) On the last trip I missed the bird by 30 minutes. Well, it took 11 years and 6,300 miles but I finally had my tern.

Today I had an absolutely fantastic day, finally getting outside the wire into the surrounding farmland on a civil affairs mission, delivering school supplies to children. Not many new birds. I was trying not to drive the humvee into an irrigation canal. I did see a few egrets in the fields (maybe cattle egrets) and a group of blue-cheeked bee-eaters hawking for insects and perching on power lines.

I've been finding a good bit of wildlife in and around our building. About a week and a half ago I found some bats living in the recesses around our drainpipes. I'm not sure what species they are— they look like North American little brown bats except they are a sandy blond color. Up to 15 bats jam into the pipe recesses and roost all day and much of the night. They seem to be most active at dusk, swooping around our lights.

Today I caught a nice brown-and-black-colored skink that ran under the air-conditioner unit. When I picked up the lizard, it promptly dropped its tail in an attempt to get away from me. I also captured a green toad today after 4 weeks of fruitless search. I could hear them calling in a ditch but I never could find them.

We've had lot of rocket and mortar attacks in
the last few days. One day we had 8 or 9 hits inside
the wire. As a result we need to go everywhere in
body armor and helmet. So Saturday was a day for
birding in "full battle rattle," weapon included,
of course.

At the laundry pond was a squacco heron
clambering around in a patch of reeds. It was a
lifer for me. Also at the pond was a big purple
swamphen. A great egret flew over while I was
checking out the barn swallows to see if there was
anything different. There wasn't. Later I went to
the pond by the junkyard, probably 2 or 3 acres of
open water surrounded by tall reeds. There was lots
of commotion in the reeds, with 5 or 6 Dead Sea
sparrows darting in and out. They are in the same
family as the house sparrow but quite a bit nois-
ier—pretty little birds. While I was watching them,
a large brown warbler hopped up on a reed. It was
my second lifer of the day, a great reed warbler.

SUNDAY, APRIL 25

Yesterday I took a long walk around base. The
weather was hot, and I didn't leave until after
lunchtime. For the first half hour I saw the usual
suspects around. Along one of the side streets near
the airstrip I found a pair of Old World warblers
hopping around in some large trees. One was
an icterine warbler; the other was some other
nondescript type of *Hippolais* species, possibly an
olivaceous warbler. While I was thumbing through
my field guide, a lady came up to me and intro-
duced herself as a fellow birder. She's working
here on base as a DoD [Department of Defense]

civilian, I think. We chatted a bit about what we've seen here. She said a white-cheeked bulbul sings outside her window every morning.

I had two new birds. Out at the pond behind the laundry, five white-winged terns were cruising around the reeds. These terns breed in this area, so they might be here to stay. The other new bird was a spectacular white-breasted, or Smyrna, kingfisher, with a big red storklike bill, reddish brown head, and blue wings, back, and tail. It was very obliging, perching on the reeds in front of me.

I think I walked 4 or 5 miles. I had all my gear on and was completely soaked with sweat when I got back.

Saturday I took a late afternoon trip around the base, following the loop road down to the laundry pond. A couple of guys came over and I let them look at a purple swamphen through my binoculars. They seemed amused at me wanting to look at birds.

Coming back I passed one of the many large cement bunkers on base. On the top of the bunker twenty feet from me was a little owl. It flew away when I got out of my truck, but I came back at dusk and it was sitting in the same place.

My final stop was a marsh near the north part of post, where I had seen a jackal the day before. I parked to wait for sunset, hoping to get a better look. Bee-eaters flew back and forth making *churring* sounds. A couple common swifts and cattle egrets flew over the reeds, and black-winged stilts flew around. Just before sunset, the jackal poked its head out from behind the berm and trotted into the open. It came within 50 feet of me and stopped, then ran off into the marsh.

THURSDAY, MAY 6

A few days ago I got to go down to the Tigris River
to take water samples, and I managed to see a few
new birds.

The dirt road down to the river passed by some
clay banks. They had holes I assume were made by
all the blue-cheeked bee-eaters flying around. On
the telephone wires I saw several Indian rollers and
a white-breasted kingfisher. I also saw a hoopoe
flying near the road. They are incredibly cool birds.

The river is lined with reeds and is about 1/4
mile wide. The water was very muddy-looking.
I saw about 25 white-winged terns flying low over
the water, also a night heron slowly flying upriver.
A small, spry bird emerged out of the reeds next
to me and hopped around on a log. It was plain-
colored with a rufous tail that it held upright like
a wren. This new bird (for me) turned out to
be a rufous bush robin. One other new bird was
a European roller, flying low over me.

Today we had a sandstorm. The trees were whipping around and clouds of sand were rolling through. I found a broken wood pigeon egg at the base of a tamarisk tree, the wind having thrown it out. The pigeon was still sitting on the nest, so there were probably more. Out back I watched two house sparrows and two white-cheeked bulbuls fruitlessly chasing a large white moth.

I need to get out again soon.

Several of our personnel had to go to the far south for a site visit. One captain had to fly back by helicopter, our preferred mode of travel. It's much safer than driving these days. To avoid being a target from ground fire they fly less than 100 feet off the ground. You are closer, but you are a target for only a split second as you zip overhead.

On the way the helicopter hit a bird. It traveled through one of the windows near the pilot's feet and into the helicopter. Everyone took pictures. The bird was a male pin-tailed sandgrouse. I'd like to see one alive, maybe later this year.

The ponds remain focal points of activity. The
laundry pond is always good for a few things. Last
time I was there a purple swamphen flew from one
side of the pond to another, its bright red legs
dangling loosely underneath it. There was also
a little grebe poking around in the reeds. A few
white-winged terns are sticking around, but I
haven't seen any evidence of nesting. The standby
moorhen can usually be found patrolling the bank,
and I often see the white-breasted kingfisher.

A couple days ago I saw a spotted flycatcher
hawking for bugs in one of the tamarisk trees
behind our building. It's the first new bird I've seen
in a few weeks.

Tomorrow I'm going to take some pictures of
plants that have sprung up recently. A few species
just pop out of the baked ground and become large
in a matter of a week or two. Many are thorny or
semisucculent. It's a good idea to have some water
conservation strategy if you plan to bake in the
Iraqi sun.

May

The summer heat has come. High temperature is between 105 and 122 during the day. The white-cheeked bulbuls don't seem to be bothered in the least by the heat. They sing, chase each other around, and hop from branch to branch in the tamarisk trees.

Last weekend I had a mission in another location. I was hoping to see some new birds on my trip across the Tigris and out into the desert. Nothing new, but I did see about 10 each of both European and Indian rollers. They seemed to like roosting on the power lines next to the road. We also had quite a few blue-cheeked bee-eaters swooping over the fields.

The wood pigeons are still to be found everywhere. They have a funny bounding flight sometimes—almost like they're doing it for fun. They power up at a 45-degree angle, then swoop down with wings bent downward. They repeat this so the flight path is in the shape of a sine wave (or cosine, depending on where you start).

Out in the desert I watched a crested lark hovering about 100 feet off the ground, singing its heart out. The amazing thing is that it kept it up for almost 10 minutes, slowly drifting in its hover. Finally it came flying down and rested on the ground near me.

The camp I visited was so quiet compared to where I live. No din of a generator around every corner and no light pollution from streetlights. I sat outside for a long time watching the stars. I saw 3 shooting stars.

On my way down to the clinic today I noticed that one of the date palms next to the road has a great load of fruit. (Each female tree can produce 150 pounds a season.) The fruit needs the extreme summer heat to ripen. The Iraqis call the date palm *nakal*, and it holds a special place in their national identity. Palm fronds are a common symbol on money, on government seals, etc. Date groves are everywhere in the river valleys, the trees growing quite tall (up to 30 meters). The scientific name is *Phoenix dactylifera*—and like the mythical bird rising out of the ashes, millions of these trees rise out of the scorching Iraqi countryside.

There is a saying that a date palm must have its feet in running water and its head in the fire of the sky. There were once 30 million trees in the country. The combined effects of the Iran-Iraq war and Saddam's draining of the southern marshes reduced the number by half.

Got out for four hours on Saturday from 1730–2130. The temperature was over 110 when I started near the north pond. Dead Sea sparrows were flying around in the tamarisk trees near the edge of the reeds. As I was watching some wood pigeons, a pair of F-16s came tearing down the runway with their afterburners going. The noise was incredible as they quickly disappeared into the sky. The birds were unfazed.

JUNE

Eventually I made it down to my main birding spot, the laundry pond. As sunset approached the birds got more active. Half a dozen black-winged stilts chased each other all over, calling like terns the whole time. Out in the pond I had fantastic views of a whiskered tern wheeling around and plucking food out of the water. And I finally picked out a pair of red-rumped swallows, after scrutinizing hundreds of barn swallows since spring.

There are a few birds I thought I would have seen by now, but haven't. Chief among them is the white stork. It could be that my location just doesn't have good habitat. I was talking to one of our local guys, quizzing him on the Arabic names of various birds and animals. He said the white stork is called *lak-lak*. They nest on the tops of several mosques in a nearby town. As in the West, the stork is associated with bringing babies. Some of the guys started singing me a local song about the stork, a mother, and a baby.

This morning I had a relaxing walk down to the pond. We had cloud cover, which was unusual. It kept the temperature below 90 until I got back around 8:45 a.m. Often it is already 100+ by then.

I stopped to examine a plant I haven't yet identified. They started coming up in late April and are still going strong, becoming fairly large bushes with semisucculent leaves. They produce small fruit that look like tiny watermelons, and when ripe split open into four sections, revealing red flesh with little black seeds.

I've got to get out and drive the roads at night more. A few nights ago, around 3 a.m., I picked up a few of our soldiers who came in from Baghdad. Afterward, I saw 2 jackals skulking up the road and a long-eared hedgehog scurrying around by the side of the road. It looked like a prickly little white hovercraft, its feet moving so fast that it seemed to be floating above the ground.

Another short visit to the laundry pond. A pickup truck was circling the pond, which flushed some birds out of the reeds and into the open water. About 20 little grebes congregated on one end of the pond. I haven't seen so many of these birds congregated before. Other birds that seemed to be flushed out were a few moorhens, a single purple swamphen, and a pair of marbled teals.

Also out in the open water I saw 16 white-winged black terns feeding. From what I've observed, the terns are here mostly in the morning and evening. During the heat of the day I think they fly back to the Tigris River, about 2 miles away. Near the edge of the pond I saw a beautiful butterfly that turned out to be a blue pansy *(Junonia orithya)*. Several subspecies are found from the Middle East through South Asia to Australia.

I've taken a 6,200-mile change in venue for a few weeks. I'm back in the northeast U.S. for R & R, so my observations in the last week have been all North American. I'll be back in Iraq soon enough.

Yesterday I sat on my back deck listening to an Eastern wood pewee and a red-eyed vireo singing in the woods behind my house. A ruby-throated hummingbird has been frequenting the flowers. The feeder is playing host to white-breasted nut-hatches, black-capped chickadees, chipping sparrows, American goldfinch, house sparrows, tufted titmice, and a Carolina wren. I've seen a few barn swallows and chimney swifts flying above.

My kids and I took a drive yesterday and stopped by a large field to watch a coyote padding around. We also took a hike in the woods a few days ago and found flowering Indian pipes. We collected a big variety of mushrooms and brought them home to make spore prints. The goldenrod have started to flower, a sure sign that summer is half over.

Back in Iraq. I got out for a little while on Saturday, visited the usual places. One of the ponds had over 100 white-winged black terns, happily feeding over the water or roosting on little islands in the middle. No migrant shorebirds, but I did see the resident black-winged stilts as well as half a dozen little egrets. At one of the other ponds I saw a turtle dove, the first I've seen here. It should be a common breeder in central Iraq but I have a feeling there are a few common birds I'm missing because of my limited mobility.

The Syrian mesquite plants that were just green feathery sprouts in March are now one- to two-foot bushes with fat orange pods all over their tops. In the spring I saw some old blackened pods and thought they were insect galls.

At one of the ponds I startled a golden jackal that was drinking at a pipe draining into the sulfur-smelling water. I was only about 20 feet away when it saw me. It ran about 50 feet and stopped, turning to get a good look.

My four-day trip to some other
bases was very productive.
On the helicopter to Baghdad
I saw dozens of cattle egrets
flying over fields and canals,
and groups of spur-winged and
red-wattled plovers in the fields. We were flying
below 100 feet most of the time so the sightseeing
was fantastic.

I stayed the first day at a palace complex near
Baghdad with a few large lakes. (I stayed in a
trailer.) Friday morning I walked a three-mile loop
around the large lake. Unlike the salt ponds of my
base, these lakes were fresh and had fish in them,
jumping in the early morning. At a small canal
leading into the lake I watched a black-and-white
pied kingfisher hover over the water, dive down
to catch a small fish, then fly back to its perch and
flip the fish in its bill and down its throat. A couple
white-cheeked bulbuls chased each other in the
trees nearby.

My first new bird of the trip was a pygmy cormorant; I saw a few throughout the day, flying back and forth over the lake. On the far side I saw a moorhen walking near the water and a few graceful prinia hopping around in the bushes. A pair of hooded crows flew over me and landed on the perimeter fence, making a croaking call.

The same day we made the trek down to a base near the ruins of ancient Babylon. The place I stayed was right next to the Euphrates, which is significantly smaller than the Tigris. We ate dinner on the river. The Polish soldiers threw pieces of bread into the river, and big schools of fish, probably some type of cyprinid, made the water look like it was boiling as they rushed to grab a piece. After dinner I drove to the top of an artificial hill where Saddam had built a palace overlooking the ruins. The sun was setting, and I started noticing large bats pouring out of the upper floors.

The next morning I birded in the ruins of Babylon proper. My first new bird there was an Iraq babbler, which sat obligingly on a fence for a few minutes before diving into the reeds. In the same area I saw a few young white-cheeked bulbuls, just fledging. A pond near an amphitheater from Alexander the Great's time had a black-crowned night heron, a few little egrets, pied kingfishers, and black-winged stilts. Near the ruins I saw my first laughing dove, walking around near the base of a date tree. I really enjoyed the combination of the lush surroundings, the birds, and the history of Babylon—not to mention that the base is much safer than mine, almost never getting attacked.

The migrants have begun coming through in earnest. I'll get out as often as I can during the fall migration. You never know what might show up. This morning, down at the usual laundry pond, I saw three different species of shrikes!

The water is lower than it has been in a while. For the first time I saw mallards as well as a small group of marbled teal. There were more bee-eaters than usual, flying straight up in the air, then diving down to their perches. Common babblers were running among the Syrian mesquite. They reminded me of desert thrashers in the western U.S.

I found where the little owl has been roosting. When I approached, it flew into a tiny slot in one of the cement fuel bunkers. It was apparent by all the feathers in the hole that the owl spends a lot of time there. Little owls are often out during the day and perch in the same place day after day. I've seen this one a couple times, sitting on the exact same light pole.

There seem to be fewer terns at the pond this week but the numbers of little egret continue to increase. I counted 37 one day. I saw a small flock of garganey, the first so far. All were either females or drakes in eclipse plumage. There also have been a few coot, some more mallards and marbled teal.

The large lakes in central Iraq have traditionally been the wintering grounds of large numbers of waterfowl. I read somewhere that 30,000 coot were sold one winter for food in the markets of Fallujah, which is nestled between two large lakes.

Recently I've had some fantastic views of hoopoe, certainly one of the most unique birds I've seen here. In flight they almost look like a broad-winged woodpecker with their striking black-and-white wings. Their body is a buff color and they have a crest they can move up and down. One day a hoopoe landed about 50 feet from me at the edge of the pond, and I spent 10 minutes watching it hop around in the mud, catching insects and every so often stopping, cocking its head to one side, and erecting the crest in its full glory. Some local people believe that the hoopoe, or *hud-hud*, has magical powers—its bones are used in potions and magical charms.

MONDAY, SEPTEMBER 20

Today we had a nice wind out of the north.
Around 10 a.m. I saw the first of 4 species of
migrating raptors; unfortunately I could positively
identify only one of them, a Eurasian kestrel. I saw
an eagle (most likely a spotted eagle), a buteo of
some sort, and an accipiter, either a Eurasian
sparrowhawk or a Levant sparrowhawk.

I sat on our roof for about an hour hoping
to see more raptors. Just as I was about to leave, I
looked up and saw a flock of 45 white storks riding
a thermal, never once flapping their wings as they
spiraled up higher and higher.

The migrants continue to come through. My Iraq list will soon be over 100 species. On the far side of the base next to a modular water-treatment plant is a new small pond, dug this spring. When I checked it out there was a nice selection of shorebirds, including a life bird for me: a great snipe. All were very cooperative. I drove my humvee right up to the bank and watched them from 20 feet away.

At the laundry pond I saw another new species, a group of three ferruginous ducks. The males are all reddish brown with a white belly and white on their wings when they fly. I also saw some sand martins (bank swallows) for the first time in Iraq.

Driving around the perimeter I checked the flooded areas near the fence for more shorebirds, turning up some red-wattled plovers and my third new bird of the day: a white-tailed plover.

SEPTEMBER

Today I had to go to a meeting at one of the high-security buildings. For the last two weeks I've seen a bunch of small hairstreak butterflies flying around one of the bushes outside. But because of the location I can't catch one to ID it, and I can't bring in a camera to photograph it. The butterflies have tiger-striped underwings and little black tails on their back wings.

A new bird I saw a couple of days ago was a male redstart, hopping around in the tamarisk trees near our building. Out on our patio a few nights ago, a barn owl flew in circles over us, screeching. The noise flushed a couple of wood pigeons out of our eucalyptus tree.

This morning I spent an hour watching the lunar eclipse. We were fortunate in Iraq to see totality around 5:23 a.m., when it was still dark. While still a few degrees above the horizon the eclipsed moon turned a dark reddish orange and faded into the brightening morning sky.

The rooks have officially arrived in numbers. These very social crows will be spending the winter. At dawn for the past two mornings, great scraggly flocks of rooks mixed with a few jackdaws poured over our base, moving from their roosts to the freshly plowed fields. Around noon I saw a huge kettle of several hundred rooks circling upward in a thermal. For a few minutes it was a perfect cylinder of circling black birds 50 feet wide and a couple hundred feet high. A rook tornado.

OCTOBER

A few days ago I traveled up north to a forward
operating base near Mosul. Flying low through
the lush agricultural lands bordering the Tigris, I
watched hundreds of egrets along with small flocks
of rooks and hooded crows. The most exciting bird
of the flight was a Houbara bustard, flying up from
the dry desert scrub showing large white patches
on its wings. These game birds are sometimes
hunted with trained falcons in Arab countries.

The base was very remote, with flat rocky
desert in every direction as far as the eye could see.
The trees on base were the only ones for miles, so
I thought they would make a good migrant trap. In
a bush near one of the buildings I found a redstart
and a male European robin, showing off its bright
orange breast. In another group of bushes a chiffchaff was hopping around.

On my way back we flew around Mosul. The
Tigris River loops through the city. The broad
shallows and vegetation along the river and in the
rocky hills look like very good places for birding.

The last few days have been slow on observations because I injured my knee in a soccer tournament. In the meantime, I've enjoyed watching the antics of the rooks. They are much more playful than crows and jackdaws and much more acrobatic. One sat in our big eucalyptus tree and made a racket while we were trying to hold a formation.

Though we had some wood pigeons here all summer, large flocks have returned to our base.

We've had a lot of rain the last week. I'm wondering if all the water will stimulate some new plants to come up. In Kuwait last winter the rains created a green haze of grasses on the dunes, which the camels like to snack on.

A short drive around in the middle of the day. The laundry pond had a few coots and a couple of moorhens. There was a strong wind, which seemed to keep a lot of the birds down.

In a field outside the perimeter I saw a flock of about 50 small birds flying around, then landing in a grassy area. Back home I wouldn't hesitate to call it a flock of American pipits. Here there are many more choices, and they were a little too far away to say anything, other than they were probably some type of brown pipit with white outer tail feathers. It would have been nice to have a scope. Hopefully they'll stick around and next time be on my side of the fence.

Near the dump I stopped for a look at the flock of gulls, which now number around a hundred. Like last winter, the majority were black-headed gulls, now in their white winter plumage.

This morning I walked out our back door and saw a few small birds hopping around in the top of a large eucalyptus next to our building. I climbed up on the roof to get a better look and found that it was a group of Eurasian siskins, feeding on the seeds in the eucalyptus nuts. They are pretty little birds that look like our pine siskins, with bright yellow wing bars, black caps, and yellow-streaked breasts. I spent about 10 minutes watching them feed, often hanging upside down. Even though the eucalyptus trees look like they have a bumper crop of gum nuts, these are the first birds I've seen feeding on them. Perhaps other birds can't get the seeds out of the small holes in the cone.

I haven't been for a good long walk for several weeks. Tomorrow morning I'll have an opportunity. I'll consider it a Christmas Bird Count. Because of this deployment I've missed the last two counts with my local Audubon society, which I have participated in since I was 14. The first CBC I went on, I remember seeing a flock of pine grosbeaks in the snow. We also take our annual trip to the dump—at least I can replicate the dump trip here. At home I usually get to count birds at a huge American crow roost. Here I have my rooks.

Last week on a run to the helipad I saw a little Ruppell's fox by the roadside. As we passed it turned and ran off into the bushes, flashing its very fine tail. Our force protection guys are constantly cursing the holes that the foxes and jackals dig under our perimeter fence. There's too much good stuff inside the wire; nothing is going to stop them coming in.

My CBC was somewhat abbreviated because several projects were sprung on me in the last few days. I only hit two spots, our laundry pond and the dump. I'm traveling again this week and will post after I get back. Hoping to do some birding while I'm away.

Here's my Christmas Count list:

Little grebe   2
Cattle egret   4
Grey heron   1
Mallard   7
Shoveler   4
Ferruginous duck   1
Marsh harrier   1
Moorhen   3
Coot   11
Black-headed gull   1500
Lesser black-backed gull   2
Yellow-legged gull   3

Armenian gull   8
Rock dove   200
Collared dove   18
Crested lark   7
White wagtail   12
White-cheeked bulbul   3
Graceful prinia   6
Common babbler   1
Jackdaw   12
Rook   65
Hooded crow   9
House sparrow   35

Just back from a mission down south near Nasiriyah. I was able to visit the ruins of the ancient Sumerian city of Ur. The land around there was rocky desert, much different from the fertile river valley around my home base. Several large desert bushes had started to produce pretty small pink flowers, and some fine tamarisk trees grew near the pond. I saw a nice male black redstart of the semi-rufous race.

Spent ten minutes watching a trio of pied kingfishers hunting. One caught a fat six-inch fish and beat it against a no-swimming sign for several minutes, trying to get it to stop struggling. It then gingerly flipped the fish around and swallowed it head first.

White wagtails and crested larks were everywhere, the larks running around in the parking lots and the wagtails preferring the edge of the pond.

Around the Ziggurat of Ur I saw a large eagle (*Aquila* species) and a pied wheatear, hunting from its perch on a telephone line.

All over the post, in ditches and patches of dirt next to the road, plants are coming up, encouraged by the rain. They will sprout, flower, produce seeds, and die all before the end of May. It's funny seeing patches of bright green where there has been only brown for 7 months. It's amazing the seeds survived the summer, when the ground temperature can be over 150 degrees and everything turns to a desiccated dust.

The reeds around the pond are now dead and brown. Out on the water were about 30 coots, some shovelers, a few mallards, and a pair of ferruginous ducks. A marsh harrier was cruising the perimeter. On my way back, a male siskin flew down to a puddle just in front of me, and a flock of 8 Eurasian goldfinch landed in a eucalyptus. I had great looks at these very pretty birds.

THURSDAY, JANUARY 20

Yesterday I had the use of a vehicle for the first time in almost a month. Most of our vehicles got shipped south, leaving me to hoof it. I spent time driving around to the good birding spots on base, including a few that are too far to walk to.

The laundry pond was filled with hundreds of birds. Most of the ducks were shovelers. There was a good number of common teal and coots and a few mallards. No ferruginous ducks, though I saw a small flock there the day before. Two female marsh harriers cruised the edge of the pond. A huge transport plane flew over during takeoff, putting the shovelers to flight. They wheeled around the pond a few times, then came back for a landing on the water. I also saw the first barn swallow of the year. Spring must be around the bend.

Later in the day I took along another sergeant who was interested in birding. At a third drainage pond we found more shovelers, coot, and a couple moorhens, also a purple swamphen preening itself in the reeds. I made an abortive attempt to examine some large round nests down in the bushes. Instead of getting to the nests I sank in the mud and got filthy. Each boot probably weighed 5 pounds with all the mud.

Down near the water's edge we saw a little chestnut bird with a dark cap and eyeline, skulking around like a wren. It reminded me a little of a marsh wren back home. It turned out to be a moustached warbler, a lifer for me.

THURSDAY, JANUARY 27

Yesterday was my last day in Iraq for this deployment. The last few days I walked around base quite a bit. Seeing my familiar favorite birds that I'll always remember when I think of Iraq. Residents like the playful white-cheeked bulbuls, the crested larks with no fear of people, and the hooded crows, plus winter visitors like the rooks and the ducks in the laundry pond.

The moustached warbler turned out to be my last lifer in Iraq.

I have been blessed with the opportunity to be here, doing a mission I believe in. Because of my job and the places I visited, I had perhaps more opportunity to see and appreciate Iraq's natural world than some. One day I hope to return, with binoculars but without a weapon.

I took a last nostalgic walk while waiting for our plane to Kuwait. Up by the burning dump several hundred starlings were milling around, as well as flocks of house sparrows. It's funny, I've only seen starlings four times here. On a mound of dirt by the burn pit a few dozen collared doves were roosting, some very dark with soot. A pair of kestrels patrolled the dump, using the light poles as lookouts. Across from the dump, in a rain pool by the road, 5 black-winged stilts waded around feeding. They are another beautiful bird that I'll remember well. On any day of the year I could find at least a few somewhere in our camp.

I continued up to a large drainage pond, where I found a pair of magpies hopping around a large bush calling to each other. I also saw a few coots and a purple swamphen near the edge of the reeds. A moorhen called from inside the reeds, then flew across the pond.

Night fell and I boarded a C-130 for the flight to Kuwait.

This will be my last entry from the Middle East.
We are about to make our way back home via
snowy Fort Drum, New York. My next entry may
be about wild turkeys and white-tailed deer, both
plentiful there. A couple days ago, on my way to
the PX, I saw what might be my last lifer, a brown-
necked raven soaring over Camp Doha.

Today I spent about an hour watching Libyan
jirds, a kind of large gerbil that lives in the dunes.
I've been looking in holes in the dunes hoping
to see one, and today I decided I'd go out before
sunset, just sit in the dunes and wait for the
jirds to come out to feed. Within 5 minutes they
were hopping around, eating seeds, running into
one hole and coming out another 20 feet away.
Their tails are incredibly long, reddish at the base
and tipped with a black tuft, sticking straight up
in the air when they run. Very cool little beasts.

As I walked over the jirds' dunes, I saw a pure
white dove circle over the camp. I'll take it as a
good omen.

KEY TO THE ILLUSTRATIONS

 Barn swallow (right), 37
Hirundo rustica

Red-rumped swallow (left), 37
Hirundo daurica

 Black-headed gull, 3, 56
Larus ridibundus

 Black-winged stilt, 13, 42
Himantopus himantopus

 Blue-cheeked bee-eater, 24
Merops superciliosus

Pied kingfisher, 44
Ceryle rudis

Purple swamphen, 32, 62
Porphyrio porphyrio

Rook, 19, 52
Corvus frugilegus

Shoveler, 59
Anas clypeata

White-cheeked bulbul, 34
Pycnonotus leucogenys

White stork, 38
Ciconia ciconia

Wood pigeon, 55
Columba palumbus

MY LIFE LIST FROM IRAQ

This list includes all 122 species I saw in Iraq or Kuwait, with selective annotation. The unabridged list can be found at http://birdingbabylon. blogspot.com/. LSAA is LSA Anaconda, my home base.

GREBES & CORMORANTS

Little grebe, *Tachybaptus ruficollis*
> Many seen throughout the year in small reed-fringed pond on LSAA, Salah ad Dihn Province. Up to 20 seen at one time in July.

Great-crested grebe, *Podiceps cristatus*
> One individual at LSAA, September 2004.

Great cormorant, *Phalacrocorax carbo*
> Flock of about 25 migrating north along Tigris River.

Pygmy cormorant, *Phalacrocorax pygmaeus*
> Individuals in late summer and fall in lakes around Camp Victory.

HERONS, EGRETS & STORKS

Black-crowned night heron, *Nycticorax nycticorax*
> Individuals or pairs seen at ponds on LSAA, Camp Liberty, Victory Base, Babylon ruins, and the Tigris River in Salah ad Dihn Province.

Squacco heron, *Ardeola ralloides*
> Seen during spring and early summer on LSAA, and sometimes on helicopter runs between Baghdad and LSAA.

Cattle egret, *Bubulcus ibis*
> Common resident of Tigris Valley, often seen in large flocks over agricultural lands on flights to Baghdad.

Little egret, *Egretta garzetta*
> Individuals throughout the year, large numbers in late summer to early fall. Up to 37 seen at the LSAA laundry pond.

Great egret, *Ardea alba*

Grey heron, *Ardea cinerea*
> Single birds seen in winter at LSAA and at Ali Base (Tallil) near Nasiriyah.

Purple heron, *Ardea purpurea*
> Flock of about 25 migrating north along Tigris River.

White stork, *Ciconia ciconia*
> A flock of 45 migrating birds seen in late September over LSAA circling in a thermal for 10 minutes before moving south.

DUCKS & GEESE

Common teal, *Anas crecca*
> Up to 20 present at LSAA ponds in January 2005. Many small ducks seen during winter may have been this species.

Mallard, *Anas platyrhynchos*
> Seen in small flocks at LSAA pond from September to January.

Garganey, *Anas querquedula*
> Seen in small numbers throughout fall and winter.

Shoveler, *Anas clypeata*
> First seen March 2004 during migration; again at LSAA starting in September. Flocks of several hundred present in January 2005.

Marbled teal, *Marmaronetta angustirostris*
> Small numbers of this globally threatened species seen on my base all spring and summer. May have bred, but I never saw any young.

Ferruginous duck, *Aythya nyroca*

KITES, OLD WORLD VULTURES, HAWKS & EAGLES

Black kite, *Milvus migrans*

Egyptian vulture, *Neophron percnopterus*
> Two birds described by another soldier were most likely this species. Seen feeding on the ground on LSAA, spring 2004.

Marsh harrier, *Circus aeruginosus*
> Two birds spent much of the winter hunting in the reedbeds of LSAA's drainage ponds.

European sparrowhawk, *Accipiter nisus*
> A migrating accipiter seen in late September was either this or a closely related species like the Levant goshawk.

Buzzard sp., *Buteo buteo*
> A late September migrant on LSAA was likely a common buzzard.

Greater spotted eagle, *Aquila clanga*
> A large Aquila species circling the ruins of Ur in southern Iraq was probably this species.

FALCONS

Lesser kestrel, *Falco naumanni*

Kestrel, *Falco tinnunculus*

Resident on LSAA, often seen hunting over marshes and fields.

Merlin, *Falco columbarius*

One spent several days hunting at the LSAA dump, in January 2005.

Hobby, *Falco subbuteo*

A small, dark, streaked falcon seen in October 2004 at Al Asad Airbase
in Al Anbar Province was likely this species.

Saker falcon, *Falco cherrug*

A brown migrating falcon seen at LSAA may have been this species.

PHEASANTS, QUAILS & ALLIES

Black francolin, *Francolinus francolinus*

I watched two spectacular males chasing each other in scrub on the
southern part of Camp Victory near Baghdad International Airport.

Common quail, *Coturnix coturnix*

One bird flushed from the grass in fields abutting LSAA.

RAILS, COOTS & ALLIES

Common moorhen, *Gallinula chloropus*

Year-round resident in the largest two ponds at LSAA. I saw several
black fuzzy chicks during summer.

Purple swamphen, *Porphyrio porphyrio*

Large bird with long red legs, resident in the largest pond on LSAA.
More often heard than seen, preferring to stay hidden in the reeds.

Coot, *Fulica atra*

Fall and winter visitor at LSAA.

BUSTARDS

Macqueen's bustard, *Chlamydotis macqueenii*

One seen from a helicopter while flying from Balad to FOB Endurance
over scrub. Formerly considered a subspecies of the Houbara bustard.

AVOCETS & STILTS

Pied avocet, *Recurvirostra avosetta*

Seen in roadside ponds and once at LSAA.

Black-winged stilt, *Himantopus himantopus*
    One of the most common and distinctive birds on LSAA, often seen
    in noisy flocks at any standing water.

PLOVERS & LAPWINGS
Common ringed plover, *Charadrius hiaticula*
Kentish (snowy) plover, *Charadrius alexandrinus*
    Birds seen at Tallil Airbase, now Ali Base, near Nasiriyah.
Spur-winged plover, *Vanellus spinosus*
Red-wattled plover, *Vanellus indicus*
    Noisy breeding residents throughout the Tigris and Euphrates valleys.
Sociable plover, *Vanellus gregarius*
    Possible sighting of a flock of this globally threatened species from a
    helicopter in the farmland north of LSAA.
White-tailed plover, *Vanellus leucurus*

SANDPIPERS & ALLIES
Common snipe, *Gallinago gallinago*
Great snipe, *Gallinago media*
    One bird seen resting at the edge of a sewage pond on LSAA.
Black-tailed godwit, *Limosa limosa*
    Several wintering birds seen at CSC Scania, February 2004.
Ruff, *Philomachus pugnax*
    Multiple birds seen in roadside ponds near Tallil Airbase.
Spotted redshank, *Tringa erythropus*
Common redshank, *Tringa totanus*
    One of the most common wintering sandpipers seen on LSAA and in
    roadside ponds south of Baghdad.
Green sandpiper, *Tringa ochropus*
Wood sandpiper, *Tringa glareola*
Common sandpiper, *Actitis hypoleucos*

GULLS & TERNS
Black-headed gull, *Larus ridibundus*
    Large wintering flocks of up to 500 birds fed at the LSAA dump.
Slender-billed gull, *Larus genei*
    One individual swimming in a roadside pond near Diwaniya.

Lesser black-backed gull, *Larus fuscus*
Yellow-legged (Caspian) gull, *Larus cachinnans*
Armenian gull, *Larus armenicus*
Common tern, *Sterna hirundo*
Little tern, *Sterna albifrons*
> Seen once on LSAA at laundry pond. Breeds elsewhere in river valleys.

Whiskered tern, *Chlidonias hybridus*
> Seen throughout the spring and summer on the ponds at LSAA.

White-winged tern, *Chlidonias leucopterus*
> Summer visitor to Tigris and Euphrates valleys. Common visitor to LSAA ponds. Over a hundred gathered there in late summer.

SANDGROUSE, DOVES & PIGEONS

Pin-tailed sandgrouse, *Pterocles alchata*
> A male struck a helicopter coming back from Baghdad.

Rock dove, *Columba livia*
Wood pigeon, *Columba palumbus*
> Thousands of these large pigeons can be found on LSAA and in nearby area. Many seem to favor the date palm groves.

Collared dove, *Streptopelia decaocto*
> Common resident breeder on LSAA and throughout central Iraq.

Turtle dove, *Streptopelia turtur*
Laughing dove, *Streptopelia senegalensis*

OWLS

Little owl, *Athena noctua*
> Seen several times on LSAA. Active during the day.

Barn owl, *Tyto alba*
> Resident breeder on LSAA and elsewhere.

SWIFTS & KINGFISHERS

Common swift, *Apus apus*
> A migrating pair seen in spring near an LSAA drainage pond.

White-breasted kingfisher, *Halcyon smyrnensis*
> Resident breeder in Tigris and Euphrates River valleys. Seen often at LSAA ponds, more common in nearby village.

Pied kingfisher, *Ceryle rudis*
> Seen feeding in ponds at Camps Victory, Liberty, and Slayer near Baghdad Airport, and along the Tigris and Euphrates.

BEE-EATERS & ROLLERS
Blue-cheeked bee-eater, *Merops superciliosus*
> Very active and beautiful green birds, seen at LSAA ponds, along canals in nearby villages, and in many other places.

European roller, *Coracias garrulus*
> Seen on fenceline at LSAA and on powerlines on the road to Khalis.

Indian roller, *Coracias benghalensis*

HOOPOES
Hoopoe, *Upupa epops*
> Seen near laundry pond at LSAA and in villages during migration.

LARKS, SWALLOWS & MARTINS
Crested lark, *Galerida cristata*
> A very tame and distinctive bird seen in many habitats from barren desert to lush river valleys. Some hung around the dining halls.

Sand martin (bank swallow), *Riparia riparia*

Barn swallow, *Hirundo rustica*
> Very common summer breeder. First migrants seen in January.

Red-rumped swallow, *Hirundo daurica*

WAGTAILS, PIPITS & BULBULS
Yellow wagtail, *Motacilla flava*
> Several sightings near water on LSAA during migration.

Grey wagtail, *Motacilla cinerea*

White wagtail, *Motacilla alba*
> Common winter visitor throughout Iraq and Kuwait. Very tame.

White-cheeked bulbul, *Pycnonotus leucogenys*
> A distinctive bird seen throughout the Tigris and Euphrates valleys.

GRASS WARBLERS & OLD WORLD WARBLERS
Graceful prinia, *Prinia gracilis*
> Very active little bird, common at LSAA and other camps.

Moustached warbler, *Acrocephalus melanopogon*
    One seen in marshy area on LSAA, January 2005.
Great reed warbler, *Acrocephalus arundinaceus*
    One migrant singing in the reeds, northwest drainage pond on LSAA.
Icterine warbler, *Hippolais icterina*
Desert warbler, *Sylvia nana*
    Last species I saw in the Middle East, near Camp Victory, Kuwait.
Eastern orphean warbler, *Sylvia crassirostris*
Chiffchaff, *Phylloscopus collybita*
    One bird seen at FOB Endurance, south of Mosul.
Willow warbler, *Phylloscopus trochilus*

ROBINS, CHATS & OLD WORLD FLYCATCHERS
Spotted flycatcher, *Muscicapa striata*
    Seen on LSAA during migration in tamarisk trees or on fenceline.
Rufous bush robin, *Cercotrichas galactotes*
European robin, *Erithacus rubecula*
    Single male at FOB Endurance, near Qayarrah, October 2004.
Black redstart, *Phoenicurus ochruros*
    Common in fall and winter, seen on LSAA and elsewhere.
Common redstart, *Phoenicurus phoenicurus*
Stonechat, *Saxicola rubicola*
Northern wheatear, *Oenanthe oenanthe*
    One individual at Al Asad Airbase, Al Anbar Province, October 2004.
Isabelline wheatear, *Oenanthe isabellina*
Pied wheatear, *Oenanthe pleschanka*
    Single bird near the Ziggurat of Ur, near Nasiriyah, December 2004.
Desert wheatear, *Oenanthe deserti*
    Seen at Udari Range and Camp Virginia in Kuwait, February 2004.

BABBLERS & SHRIKES
Common babbler, *Turdoides caudatus*
    Often seen running in scrub or perched on fences at LSAA.
Iraq babbler, *Turdoides altirostris*
    Several seen at Camp Alpha, Babylon ruins, in phragmites reeds.

Isabelline shrike, *Lanius isabellinus*
    Seen at Scania near Ad Diwaniyah in February, also at Victory Base.
Red-backed shrike, *Lanius collurio*
Lesser grey shrike, *Lanius minor*
Southern grey shrike, *Lanius meridionalis*
Woodchat shrike, *Lanius senator*

MAGPIES, JAYS, CROWS & RAVENS
Magpie, *Pica pica*
    Seen year-round at LSAA, seemed more common at higher elevations.
Jackdaw, *Corvus monedula*
    Winter visitor sometimes mixed in with rook flocks.
Rook, *Corvus frugilegus*
    Winter visitors abundant late October to early spring from Baghdad
    north. Huge flocks common in agricultural areas.
Hooded crow, *Corvus corone cornix*
Mesopotamian crow, *Corvus corone capellanus*
    Year-round resident in the Tigris and Euphrates valleys.
Brown-necked raven, *Corvus ruficollis*

STARLINGS & MYNAS
Eurasian starling, *Sturnus vulgaris*
    Seen only three times, all at LSAA.

WEAVER FINCHES & FINCHES
House sparrow, *Passer domesticus*
    Abundant resident. Seen at all locations from remote desert camps to
    villages and farms in river valleys.
Spanish sparrow, *Passer hispaniolensis*
    Small flock seen migrating in spring on LSAA feeding on thistles.
Dead Sea sparrow, *Passer moabiticus*
    Noisy little birds that built globular stick nests near phragmites reeds.
Chaffinch, *Fringilla coelebs*
European goldfinch, *Carduelis carduelis*
    Migrated through in March and again in fall.
Eurasian siskin, *Carduelis spinus*
    Seen twice on LSAA, once feeding on tiny eucalyptus seeds.

ABOUT THE AUTHOR

Connecticut Army National Guardsman and Sergeant First Class Jonathan Trouern-Trend served with the 118th Area Support Medical Battalion in Iraq. Until his yearlong tour of duty ended in February 2005, he maintained an online journal documenting his birdwatching in a war zone. "The blog came out of surfing the Internet to find out more about what I was getting into before I went to Iraq," he says. "Several soldiers had blogs and I thought that would be an interesting way to keep track of what I was seeing." Trouern-Trend lives in Marlborough, Connecticut, with his wife, Nancy, and their five children. He received his B.S. in Biology from the University of Connecticut, and he currently works for the American Red Cross Blood Services in its Epidemiology and Surveillance program. He pursues his nature observations at home and wherever he travels.